Mastering Your Finances: A Comprehensive Guide to Effective Money Management and Budgeting

ISBN: 9798862229264

Financial Disclaimer

The information provided in this book, "Mastering Your Finances: A Comprehensive Guide to Effective Money Management and Budgeting," is intended for educational and informational purposes only. The author, publisher, and contributors are not financial advisors, and the content in this book should not be construed as professional financial, investment, or legal advice.

The content in this book is based on the author's knowledge and research as of the publication date. The financial landscape is dynamic and subject to change, and new developments may have occurred since the last update.

Readers are strongly encouraged to consult with qualified financial advisors, legal professionals, or other experts before making any financial, investment, or legal decisions. The author and publisher do not make any guarantees, representations, or warranties regarding the accuracy, completeness, or suitability of the information provided in this book. Any reliance on the information in this book is at the reader's own risk.

The author and publisher disclaim any liability for any direct, indirect, incidental, special, or consequential damages arising from the use of or reliance on the information in this book, or any actions or decisions made based on the content herein. The reader acknowledges that there are no promises, guarantees, or assurances of specific financial outcomes or success by implementing the strategies or recommendations presented in this book.

Furthermore, the author and publisher disclaim any responsibility for the outcomes of financial, investment, or legal decisions made by readers. Readers are encouraged to conduct their own research, due diligence, and seek professional advice when necessary.

By reading this book, the reader agrees to release, indemnify, and hold harmless the author, publisher, and contributors from any and all claims, damages, liabilities, or expenses that may arise from the reader's use of or reliance on the information contained in this book.

This disclaimer serves as a legal notice that the content of this book is for informational purposes only, and the author and publisher are not responsible for any actions or decisions made by readers based on the content herein.

Chapter 1: The Importance of Financial Literacy

Money is more than just currency; it's a tool that can either empower or restrict us. Understanding how to manage it effectively is crucial for securing our financial future. In this chapter, we'll explore the foundations of financial literacy, why it matters, and how it sets the stage for successful budgeting.

The Financial Literacy Gap

Financial illiteracy is a pervasive issue worldwide. According to a study by the Organization for Economic Co-operation and Development (OECD), only 38% of adults in developed countries are financially literate. This means that a significant portion of the population lacks the basic knowledge and skills necessary to make informed financial decisions.

Source: OECD/INFE International Survey of Adult Financial Literacy Competencies

The Consequences of Financial Ignorance

Not understanding how to manage money can have severe consequences. Consider the following:

1. Debt Accumulation: Without proper financial knowledge, many individuals find themselves accumulating debt. In the United States, the average credit card debt per borrower was $5,313 in 2020.

Source: Experian's 2020 Consumer Credit Review

2. Limited Savings: A lack of savings is another outcome. In fact, a survey by Bankrate revealed that 28% of Americans have no emergency savings at all.

Source: Bankrate's Financial Security Index

3. Stress and Anxiety: Financial stress can take a significant toll on mental health. A study by the American Psychological Association found that 72% of adults report feeling stressed about money at least some of the time.

Source: American Psychological Association's Stress in America Report

The Power of Financial Literacy

On the flip side, financial literacy empowers individuals to make sound financial decisions. Here's how it can transform your life:

1. Informed Decision-Making: Financial literacy equips you with the knowledge to make informed choices about saving, investing, and spending.

2. Debt Management: Understanding how credit works can help you avoid high-interest debt and pay off existing loans faster.

3. Building Wealth: Financial literacy enables you to grow your wealth over time, leading to financial security and opportunities for your future.

4. Achieving Your Goals: Whether you dream of owning a home, traveling the world, or retiring comfortably, financial literacy is your compass to reach these goals.

Steps to Boost Your Financial Literacy

1. **Start with the Basics:** Begin by learning essential financial concepts such as budgeting, saving, and investing. Books like "The Total Money Makeover" by Dave Ramsey and "Rich Dad Poor Dad" by Robert Kiyosaki are excellent starting points.

2. **Take Online Courses:** There are numerous free and paid online courses that cover various aspects of personal finance. Websites like Coursera, Udemy, and Khan Academy offer valuable resources.

3. **Follow Financial News:** Stay informed about the latest financial news and trends. Reading financial websites or subscribing to financial newsletters can help you stay up-to-date.

4. **Seek Professional Advice:** Consider consulting a financial advisor who can provide personalized guidance based on your financial goals and situation.

5. **Practice What You Learn:** Apply your newfound knowledge to your own finances. Create a budget, open a savings account, or start investing in a retirement fund.

Financial literacy is not an end but a means to an end – the end being financial security, freedom, and the ability to achieve your life goals. As you embark on your journey to financial mastery, remember that every step counts. In the chapters ahead, we will delve deeper into the practical aspects of managing your money, starting with the fundamental tool of financial planning: budgeting.

Chapter 2: Understanding Your Financial Landscape

Welcome to the second chapter of "Mastering Your Finances." In this chapter, we'll take a close look at your current financial situation. To successfully navigate your financial journey, you need to know where you stand. We'll explore how to assess your income, analyze your expenses, and understand the psychology of your financial decisions.

Assessing Your Current Financial Situation

Step 1: Evaluate Your Income

Your income is the lifeblood of your financial well-being. Let's begin by understanding it better.

Statistics: In the United States, the median household income was $67,521 in 2020. However, income can vary widely depending on factors like location, education, and career.

Source: U.S. Census Bureau's 2020 Income and Poverty Report

Action Steps:

1. **Gather Income Sources:** Make a list of all your income sources. This may include your salary, rental income, freelance work, or investment dividends.

2. **Calculate Your Net Income:** Subtract taxes and other deductions from your gross income to determine your net income, the amount you actually receive.

Step 2: Analyze Your Expenses

Now that we have a clearer picture of your income, it's time to dig into your expenses.

Statistics: The average American household spent $63,036 in 2020. This included expenses like housing, transportation, food, and healthcare.

Source: U.S. Bureau of Labor Statistics' Consumer Expenditure Survey

Action Steps:

1. **Categorize Your Expenses:** Create categories for your expenses, such as housing, transportation, groceries, entertainment, and debt payments.

2. **Track Your Expenses:** Keep a detailed record of your spending for a month. You can use apps like Mint or YNAB (You Need A Budget) to make this process easier.

3. **Identify Discretionary vs. Fixed Expenses:** Differentiate between fixed expenses (like rent or mortgage) and discretionary expenses (like dining out or shopping).

4. **Calculate Your Savings Rate:** Determine how much of your income is left after covering your expenses. Ideally, you should aim to save at least 20% of your income.

The Psychology of Money

Understanding the psychology behind your financial decisions is just as crucial as the numbers themselves.

Example: Sarah, a marketing manager, realizes that she often shops online when she's stressed. Understanding this behavior helps her find healthier coping mechanisms and save money.

Action Steps:

1. **Reflect on Your Money Mindset:** Consider your beliefs and attitudes towards money. Are there any habits or beliefs that might be hindering your financial progress?

2. **Set Emotional Boundaries:** Recognize emotional spending triggers, like stress or boredom, and find alternative ways to address those emotions without spending money.

3. **Practice Delayed Gratification:** Train yourself to delay immediate wants in favor of long-term financial goals. This can be as simple as waiting 24 hours before making non-essential purchases.

4. **Seek Support:** If you're struggling with managing the emotional aspects of your finances, don't hesitate to seek support from a therapist or counselor.

Understanding your financial landscape is the first step towards financial mastery. Armed with this knowledge, you're now prepared to move on to the next chapters where we'll delve into creating a budget that aligns with your

financial goals and values. Remember, your financial journey is unique, and this chapter provides the foundational tools to help you navigate it successfully.

Chapter 3: Building a Strong Financial Foundation

Welcome to the third chapter of "Mastering Your Finances." In this pivotal chapter, we'll explore how to establish a solid financial foundation. Building this foundation is crucial for achieving financial stability and reaching your financial goals.

Creating Financial Goals

Step 1: Set Clear Goals

Financial goals are your roadmap to a better financial future. Without them, it's challenging to stay motivated and make meaningful progress.

Statistics: According to a study by Fidelity, 73% of people who set financial goals feel very or extremely happy about their financial situation compared to only 28% of those without specific goals.

Source: Fidelity's Money FIT Women Study

Action Steps:

1. **Identify Short-term, Mid-term, and Long-term Goals:** Your goals should include immediate needs (e.g., paying off credit card debt), medium-term aspirations (e.g., buying a home), and long-term objectives (e.g., retiring comfortably).

2. **Make Your Goals SMART:** Ensure your goals are Specific, Measurable, Achievable, Relevant, and Time-bound. For example, instead of saying "I want

to save money," say, "I want to save $5,000 for an emergency fund within the next 12 months."

3. **Prioritize Your Goals:** Not all goals are equal. Determine which goals are most important to you and focus your efforts on those first.

Emergency Fund and Savings

Step 2: Start Building an Emergency Fund

An emergency fund acts as a financial safety net, protecting you from unexpected expenses.

Statistics: According to the Federal Reserve, in 2020, 39% of Americans wouldn't be able to cover a $400 emergency expense without borrowing money or selling something.

Source: Federal Reserve's Report on the Economic Well-Being of U.S. Households

Action Steps:

1. **Determine Your Target:** Aim to save at least three to six months' worth of living expenses in your emergency fund. Adjust this based on your personal circumstances.

2. **Start Small, but Start Now:** If you can't save the full amount immediately, start with a smaller goal, like $1,000. The key is to get started.

3. **Automate Your Savings:** Set up an automatic transfer from your checking account to your emergency fund. Treat it as a non-negotiable monthly expense.

Debt Management

Step 3: Tackle Your Debt

Debt can be a significant obstacle to building wealth. It's essential to have a strategy for paying it off.

Statistics: The average student loan debt in the United States was $37,584 per borrower in 2020.

Source: Federal Reserve's Report on the Economic Well-Being of U.S. Households

Action Steps:

1. **List Your Debts:** Make a list of all your debts, including credit cards, student loans, and personal loans. Include the total amount owed, interest rates, and minimum monthly payments.

2. **Choose a Debt Payoff Strategy:** Two popular strategies are the Debt Snowball (paying off the smallest debt first) and the Debt Avalanche (paying off the debt with the highest interest rate first). Pick the one that suits your personality and motivation.

3. **Increase Your Debt Payments:** Allocate extra money from your budget toward your debt payments. Consider using windfalls like tax refunds or work bonuses to accelerate your progress.

Building a strong financial foundation is like constructing a solid house. It takes time, effort, and careful planning, but once it's in place, you'll have the stability and confidence to move forward on your financial journey. In the next chapter, we'll dive deeper into the budgeting process, where we'll show you how to turn your financial goals into a practical plan.

Chapter 4: The Budgeting Process

Welcome to Chapter 4 of "Mastering Your Finances." Now that you've set your financial goals, established an emergency fund, and devised a plan to manage your debt, it's time to dive into the heart of effective money management: budgeting. In this chapter, we'll explore budgeting basics, how to track your income, categorize your expenses, and create a budget tailored to your unique financial situation.

Budgeting Basics

What is a Budget?

At its core, a budget is a financial plan that outlines your income and expenses over a specific period, typically monthly. Think of it as your financial GPS, guiding you toward your goals.

Statistics: A Gallup poll found that only 32% of Americans prepare a detailed written budget every month.

Source: Gallup's Survey on Budgeting Habits

Action Steps:

1. **Choose Your Budgeting Period:** Decide whether you'll create a monthly, bi-weekly, or weekly budget. Monthly budgets are common because many bills and paychecks align with this timeframe.

2. **Determine Your Income Sources:** Identify all sources of income, including your salary, side

hustles, rental income, and any other inflow of money.

3. **List Your Expenses:** Start with broad categories like housing, transportation, groceries, and entertainment. You'll break these down further in the next steps.

Tracking Your Income

Step 1: Calculate Your Monthly Income

Understanding your income is the foundation of budgeting. To get an accurate picture, consider all sources.

Example: Sarah earns $4,000 per month from her full-time job and $500 from a freelance gig, bringing her total monthly income to $4,500.

Action Steps:

1. **Gather Pay Stubs:** Collect recent pay stubs or income statements from all your income sources.

2. **Account for Irregular Income:** If you have irregular income, estimate an average monthly amount by looking at past earnings over several months.

Identifying and Categorizing Expenses

Step 2: Track and Categorize Your Expenses

Now, let's focus on your expenses. Break them down into categories for better clarity and control.

Statistics: In the U.S., housing expenses (rent or mortgage) often account for the largest portion of a household's budget, averaging around 30% of income.

Source: U.S. Bureau of Labor Statistics' Consumer Expenditure Survey

Action Steps:

1. **Review Your Bank Statements:** Go through your bank statements and receipts for the past few months to get an accurate picture of your spending habits.

2. **Categorize Expenses:** Organize your expenses into categories, such as housing, transportation, groceries, utilities, entertainment, and debt payments.

3. **Differentiate Between Fixed and Variable Expenses:** Identify which expenses remain relatively consistent each month (fixed) and which can fluctuate (variable).

Creating a Realistic Budget

Step 3: Set Spending Limits

Now that you have a clear picture of your income and expenses, it's time to create your budget.

Example: Sarah has calculated her monthly income as $4,500 and identified her expenses. She allocates $1,200 for rent, $400 for groceries, $150 for utilities, $300 for transportation, $200 for entertainment, and $500 for debt payments.

Action Steps:

1. **Allocate Funds:** Assign a specific amount to each expense category based on your priorities and needs. Make sure your total expenses do not exceed your total income.

2. **Plan for Savings:** Don't forget to allocate money for savings and investments, including contributions to your emergency fund and retirement accounts.

3. **Use Budgeting Tools:** Consider using budgeting apps like Mint, YNAB, or personal finance software to help you create and track your budget.

Remember, your budget is a dynamic tool. It's not set in stone; you can adjust it as your financial situation changes. In the next chapter, we'll explore how to stick to your budget and overcome common challenges that may arise during your financial journey. With your budget in hand, you're well on your way to taking control of your finances.

Chapter 5: Sticking to Your Budget

Welcome to Chapter 5 of "Mastering Your Finances." Now that you've created your budget, the real challenge begins: sticking to it. In this chapter, we'll explore budgeting best practices, tips for staying on track, and strategies to save and invest for your future.

Budgeting Best Practices

Step 1: Develop a Budgeting Routine

Consistency is key to successful budgeting. Establishing a routine makes it easier to stay on track.

Statistics: A study by Charles Schwab found that 59% of Americans who budgeted their money felt financially stable, compared to only 24% of those who didn't budget.

Source: Charles Schwab's Modern Wealth Survey

Action Steps:

1. **Set a Budgeting Day:** Choose a specific day each month to review and adjust your budget. Mark it on your calendar to ensure you don't forget.

2. **Use Technology:** Leverage budgeting apps and tools to streamline the process. Many apps offer automatic transaction categorization and spending alerts.

3. **Involve Your Partner:** If you share finances with a partner, schedule regular budget meetings to keep both of you on the same page.

Tips for Staying on Track

Step 2: Stay Disciplined

Budgeting requires discipline, but there are strategies to help you stick to your plan.

Example: John wants to curb his dining-out expenses. He sets a monthly dining-out limit and brings homemade lunches to work, making it easier to resist the temptation of eating out.

Action Steps:

1. **Use Cash Envelopes:** Allocate cash into envelopes for different spending categories. When the envelope is empty, you can't spend any more in that category.

2. **Automate Savings:** Set up automatic transfers to your savings and investment accounts right after payday. This way, you're less likely to spend that money impulsively.

3. **Track Your Spending Regularly:** Review your transactions frequently to ensure you're staying within your budgeted amounts. Most budgeting apps offer real-time updates.

Saving and Investing for the Future

Step 3: Secure Your Financial Future

Budgeting isn't just about managing day-to-day expenses; it's also about building wealth for the future.

Statistics: According to the Federal Reserve, 53% of Americans do not have a retirement account or pension through their employer.

Source: Federal Reserve's Report on the Economic Well-Being of U.S. Households

Action Steps:

1. **Prioritize Retirement Savings:** Make contributions to your employer-sponsored retirement plan, such as a 401(k) or open an IRA (Individual Retirement Account).

2. **Emergency Fund Growth:** As your financial situation improves, aim to increase your emergency fund to cover six to twelve months' worth of expenses.

3. **Invest Wisely:** Educate yourself about different investment options, such as stocks, bonds, and mutual funds. Consider consulting a financial advisor to help you make informed investment decisions.

Budgeting is a lifelong journey, and mastering it takes time. It's not about depriving yourself but about making conscious choices that align with your financial goals. As you continue to follow your budget and make progress toward your objectives, remember that financial freedom and security are achievable with discipline and dedication. In the next chapter, we'll delve into common budgeting challenges and how to overcome them. Stay committed, and you'll be well on your way to financial success.

Chapter 6: Dealing with Budgeting Challenges

Welcome to Chapter 6 of "Mastering Your Finances." Along your financial journey, you may encounter various challenges that can test your commitment to budgeting. In this chapter, we'll explore common hurdles and provide strategies to overcome them effectively.

Handling Unexpected Expenses

Step 1: Be Prepared

Life is unpredictable, and unexpected expenses can derail your budget. However, being prepared can make all the difference.

Statistics: The Federal Reserve reported that in 2020, 38% of adults had trouble covering a $400 emergency expense.

Source: Federal Reserve's Report on the Economic Well-Being of U.S. Households

Action Steps:

1. **Build an Emergency Fund:** Ensure you have an emergency fund with at least three to six months' worth of living expenses. This fund acts as a safety net for unexpected costs.

2. **Prioritize Savings:** In your budget, allocate a portion of your income to savings each month, specifically for unexpected expenses. This way, you're continually building your emergency fund.

3. **Assess Your Insurance:** Review your insurance policies (health, auto, home) to ensure you have adequate coverage. Insurance can protect you from significant financial losses in case of accidents or unforeseen events.

Adjusting Your Budget

Step 2: Flexibility Is Key

Budgets are not set in stone. Life circumstances change, and your budget should evolve with them.

Example: Sarah's car needed unexpected repairs, causing her transportation expenses to exceed her budget. To compensate, she reduced her dining-out budget for the month.

Action Steps:

1. **Regularly Review Your Budget:** Set aside time each month to assess your budget. Analyze your spending, income, and progress toward your financial goals.

2. **Identify Areas for Adjustment:** If you consistently overspend in one category, consider reallocating funds from another category or adjusting your budget to reflect your evolving priorities.

3. **Be Realistic:** Life happens. Don't be too hard on yourself if you need to make changes. The goal is to maintain financial stability in the long run.

Saving for Future Goals

Step 3: Stay Motivated

Long-term financial goals, like buying a home or retiring comfortably, can sometimes feel distant. Staying motivated is essential to see them through.

Statistics: A survey by Bank of America found that 55% of Americans are not confident they will reach their long-term financial goals.

Source: Bank of America's Better Money Habits Report

Action Steps:

1. **Break Down Large Goals:** Divide big financial goals into smaller, more achievable milestones. Celebrate your progress along the way.

2. **Visualize Your Goals:** Create a vision board or use financial goal-tracking apps to visualize your goals. Seeing your progress can boost motivation.

3. **Stay Informed:** Educate yourself about investments and strategies that can help you reach your goals faster. Knowledge is a powerful motivator.

4. **Share Your Goals:** Discuss your financial goals with a trusted friend or family member. Accountability and support can help you stay on track.

Remember, budgeting is a dynamic process, and it's normal to encounter challenges. The key is to adapt, stay resilient, and continue working toward your financial goals. In the next chapter, we'll explore the psychology of spending and how to make mindful financial decisions that align with your budget. Keep up the great work on your financial journey!

Chapter 7: The Psychology of Spending

Welcome to Chapter 7 of "Mastering Your Finances." In this chapter, we'll dive into the fascinating world of the psychology of spending. Understanding why we make the financial decisions we do can help you make more mindful choices and stay aligned with your budget.

Impulse Buying and How to Control It

Step 1: Recognize Impulse Spending

Impulse buying is a common financial pitfall. It's when you make unplanned purchases on a whim, often driven by emotions rather than rational thought.

Statistics: A survey by the website CreditCards.com found that 64% of Americans have made an impulse purchase.

Source: CreditCards.com's Impulse Buying Survey

Action Steps:

1. **Identify Your Triggers:** Pay attention to situations or emotions that lead to impulse spending. Common triggers include stress, boredom, and peer pressure.

2. **Practice the 24-Hour Rule:** When tempted to make an impulse purchase, wait 24 hours before buying. This gives you time to consider if it's a genuine need or just a fleeting desire.

3. **Create a Shopping List:** Before heading to the store or shopping online, make a list of what you need and stick to it.

Understanding the Influence of Advertising

Step 2: Be a Savvy Consumer

Advertisements are designed to persuade you to buy products or services. Understanding their tactics can help you resist unnecessary spending.

Example: Mary used to fall for online ads promoting discounted clothing. After learning about the influence of advertising, she unsubscribed from promotional emails and unfollowed tempting brands on social media.

Action Steps:

1. **Question Ad Claims:** Don't take advertisements at face value. Investigate claims and compare products or services to ensure you're getting the best value.

2. **Set Ad-Free Zones:** Limit your exposure to advertising by using ad-blockers online and subscribing to ad-free streaming services.

3. **Practice Mindful Consumption:** Before making a purchase, ask yourself if it aligns with your values and if it's a true need or simply a want influenced by advertising.

Mindful Spending and Value-based Budgeting

Step 3: Align Spending with Your Values

Mindful spending involves consciously directing your money toward things that truly matter to you. It's about ensuring your spending aligns with your values and priorities.

Statistics: The American Institute of CPAs found that 78% of Americans have financial regrets, with overspending on non-essential items as the top regret.

Source: American Institute of CPAs' Financial Regrets Survey

Action Steps:

1. **Define Your Values:** Take time to identify your core values and financial priorities. These might include family, education, travel, or saving for retirement.

2. **Create a Value-based Budget:** Adjust your budget to allocate more resources to the areas that matter most to you. This can help you cut spending in areas that are less important.

3. **Practice Gratitude:** Regularly reflect on what you have and the progress you've made toward your financial goals. Gratitude can reduce the desire for unnecessary spending.

Understanding the psychology of spending can empower you to make intentional financial decisions. By recognizing impulse buying triggers, becoming a critical consumer, and aligning your spending with your values, you can stay on budget and move closer to your financial goals. In the next chapter, we'll delve into practical strategies for monitoring and adjusting your budget to ensure it remains effective on your journey to financial success.

Chapter 8: Monitoring and Adjusting Your Budget

Welcome to Chapter 8 of "Mastering Your Finances." Budgeting isn't a set-it-and-forget-it process. To achieve lasting financial success, you must regularly monitor and adjust your budget as your circumstances change. In this chapter, we'll explore practical strategies for keeping your budget on track.

Regular Budget Check-ins

Step 1: Make It a Habit

Monitoring your budget should become a routine part of your financial life. Regular check-ins help you catch potential issues early and stay accountable.

Statistics: A survey by the National Foundation for Credit Counseling found that 65% of adults who maintain a budget check it at least once a week.

Source: National Foundation for Credit Counseling's Consumer Financial Literacy Survey

Action Steps:

1. **Schedule Check-in Dates:** Choose specific dates each month to review your budget. Consistency is key.

2. **Use Reminders:** Set up digital calendar reminders or alarms to prompt you to review your budget regularly.

3. **Involve Your Partner:** If you share finances with a partner, schedule budget meetings together to discuss progress and make joint decisions.

Identifying Areas for Improvement

Step 2: Be Proactive

During your budget check-ins, pay attention to areas where you might be overspending or undersaving.

Example: Tim noticed he consistently overspent on dining out. To address this, he decided to reduce his dining-out budget and allocate more to his savings goals.

Action Steps:

1. **Review Your Transactions:** Analyze your recent spending to see if it aligns with your budgeted amounts.

2. **Look for Patterns:** Identify recurring patterns, such as overspending in certain categories or areas where you consistently have leftover funds.

3. **Adjust as Needed:** If you find discrepancies, be proactive in making adjustments to your budget. This might mean cutting spending in some areas or reallocating funds to align better with your goals.

Long-term Financial Planning

Step 3: Adapt to Life Changes

Life rarely stays static, and neither should your budget. Major life events, such as job changes, marriage, or having children, can necessitate significant budget adjustments.

Statistics: According to the U.S. Bureau of Labor Statistics, the average person changes jobs about 12 times during their career.

Source: U.S. Bureau of Labor Statistics' Job Hopping Data

Action Steps:

1. **Consider Life Events:** Anticipate significant life changes and adjust your budget accordingly. For example, if you plan to start a family, budget for childcare and other related expenses.

2. **Review Your Goals:** Regularly revisit your financial goals and adjust them as needed. Your priorities may evolve over time.

3. **Emergency Adjustments:** In times of unexpected financial hardship or windfalls, adjust your budget to accommodate these changes.

Budgeting is a dynamic process that adapts to your life circumstances. By regularly monitoring your budget, proactively identifying areas for improvement, and adjusting as needed, you can ensure your budget remains effective and aligned with your financial goals. In the next chapter, we'll explore valuable resources to support your budgeting journey, including financial tools, recommended reading, and online courses. Stay committed, and you'll continue to make progress toward financial success.

Chapter 9: Resources for Your Budgeting Journey

Welcome to Chapter 9 of "Mastering Your Finances." In this chapter, we'll explore valuable resources that can enhance your budgeting skills, provide financial support, and empower you to make informed decisions on your financial journey.

Financial Tools and Apps

Step 1: Leverage Technology

There's a wide array of budgeting tools and apps available to simplify and streamline the budgeting process.

Statistics: According to a survey by The Ascent, 61% of Americans use budgeting apps or software to track their expenses.

Source: The Ascent's Survey on Budgeting Apps

Action Steps:

1. **Explore Budgeting Apps:** Consider popular budgeting apps like Mint, YNAB (You Need A Budget), Personal Capital, or PocketGuard. These apps can help you track expenses, set financial goals, and visualize your financial progress.

2. **Automate Finances:** Use automatic bill payments and scheduled transfers to ensure your budget remains on track. Many banks offer these features through their mobile apps.

3. **Stay Secure:** Be cautious when sharing personal financial information online. Use secure, reputable apps and enable two-factor authentication whenever possible.

Recommended Reading

Step 2: Educate Yourself

Books are a valuable source of financial wisdom and guidance. Here are some recommended reads to boost your financial literacy:

Example: After reading "The Millionaire Next Door" by Thomas J. Stanley and William D. Danko, Laura adopted frugal habits and increased her savings rate.

Action Steps:

1. **Visit Your Local Library:** Borrow financial books for free or explore digital lending platforms like OverDrive and Libby.

2. **Create a Reading List:** Build a list of finance-related books that interest you. Include classics like "Rich Dad Poor Dad" by Robert Kiyosaki, "The Total Money Makeover" by Dave Ramsey, and "Your Money or Your Life" by Vicki Robin and Joe Dominguez.

3. **Join a Book Club:** Consider joining or starting a financial book club with friends or colleagues. Discussing financial concepts can deepen your understanding.

Online Courses and Educational Resources

Step 3: Invest in Learning

Online courses and educational platforms offer structured learning experiences to improve your financial literacy.

Statistics: According to Coursera, their Financial Planning Specialization saw a 444% increase in enrollment during the COVID-19 pandemic.

Source: Coursera's Impact Report

Action Steps:

1. **Explore Online Courses:** Websites like Coursera, Udemy, and edX offer a wide range of financial courses, from basic budgeting to advanced investment strategies.

2. **Seek Certified Financial Planners:** Consider consulting a Certified Financial Planner (CFP) for personalized guidance. CFPs are trained professionals who can provide expert advice.

3. **Government Resources:** Many governments provide free financial education resources online. For example, in the United States, the Consumer Financial Protection Bureau (CFPB) offers tools and guides on various financial topics.

4. **YouTube and Podcasts:** Don't overlook free resources like YouTube channels and podcasts dedicated to personal finance. Channels like "The Financial Diet" and podcasts like "The Dave Ramsey Show" offer valuable insights.

By utilizing these resources, you can enhance your financial knowledge, discover effective budgeting strategies, and gain confidence in managing your money effectively. In the final chapter, we'll recap the key takeaways from this book and provide you with actionable steps to continue mastering your finances. Stay committed to your financial journey, and the rewards will be well worth the effort.

Chapter 10: Mastering Your Finances – Recap and Action Plan

Congratulations on making it to the final chapter of "Mastering Your Finances." You've come a long way on your financial journey, and now it's time to consolidate what you've learned and put it into action. This chapter will recap key takeaways and provide you with a clear action plan to continue your financial mastery.

Key Takeaways

Step 1: Reflect on Your Journey

Before we move forward, let's revisit the essential lessons from this book:

1. **Budgeting is Your Financial GPS:** A budget is not about restriction; it's a tool that empowers you to allocate your money in ways that align with your goals and values.

2. **Set Clear Goals:** Specific, measurable, and time-bound goals are essential for financial success. Whether you're saving for an emergency fund, a vacation, or retirement, having clear objectives keeps you motivated.

3. **Emergency Fund is Your Safety Net:** An emergency fund helps you weather unexpected financial storms without derailing your budget. Aim to save at least three to six months' worth of living expenses.

4. **Debt Management is Key:** Tackling high-interest debt should be a priority. Choose a debt payoff strategy and allocate extra funds to accelerate your progress.

5. **Stay Disciplined:** Consistency and discipline are the cornerstones of successful budgeting. Establish a routine for budget check-ins and stay vigilant against impulse spending.

6. **Mindful Spending is Empowering:** Understanding the psychology of spending helps you make conscious decisions about your finances. Mindful spending ensures your money aligns with your values.

7. **Monitor and Adjust:** Regularly review and adjust your budget to accommodate changes in your life and financial goals.

8. **Leverage Resources:** Use financial tools and apps, read recommended books, take online courses, and seek guidance from experts to enhance your financial knowledge.

Your Action Plan

Step 2: Chart Your Path Forward

Now, let's create a concrete plan for your financial future:

Action Steps:

1. **Review Your Financial Goals:** Take a moment to revisit your financial goals. Are they still relevant, or have they evolved? Update them as needed.

2. **Commit to Regular Budget Check-ins:** Schedule monthly budget check-ins on your calendar and set reminders. Consistency is the key to success.

3. **Leverage Technology:** If you haven't already, explore budgeting apps and tools to streamline your financial management.

4. **Read and Learn:** Choose at least one financial book or online course to enhance your financial literacy. Make a list of books or courses that interest you.

5. **Build a Support Network:** Consider joining a financial book club or online community where you can discuss financial topics and share experiences with like-minded individuals.

6. **Consult a Financial Advisor:** If your financial situation is complex or you have specific financial goals like retirement or investing, seek advice from a Certified Financial Planner (CFP).

7. **Stay Motivated:** Continuously remind yourself of your financial goals. Visualize your progress and celebrate milestones along the way.

Your Financial Journey

Your journey to mastering your finances is ongoing. It's not about reaching a final destination but about embracing financial empowerment, making informed decisions, and achieving your goals.

Remember, setbacks may occur, but with discipline and a strong foundation, you have the tools to overcome them. Stay committed to your financial well-being, adapt to life's changes, and continue to educate yourself. Financial mastery is within your reach, and every step you take brings you closer to a brighter financial future.

Thank you for joining us on this journey. We wish you the very best in your pursuit of financial success and empowerment.

www.ingramcontent.com/pod-product-compliance
Lightning Source LLC
Chambersburg PA
CBHW072218290526
45794CB00007B/2794